James Adams

D1358055

Introduction

Welcome to the **Absolutely Awesome Terraria Quiz**!

This book is jam-packed with hundreds of questions about your favorite game. If you are looking for more information about the game or if you want to increase your own knowledge about the game then you need to grab this book now.

By finding out more and more about the game you will enjoy it more and also become more knowledgeable than your friends. If you want to become the ultimate Terraria player than you need to know about every aspect of the game!

This book has 500 questions and answers based on lots of different categories. You can test your own knowledge and then challenge your friends – see who can get the most right in the shortest time. Find out who knows the most about all the little details! Go through once then try again – go for the perfect score!

This book contains all the answers as well that will get you to being an excellent player – increase your knowledge, have fun and get a lot more out of the game.

Get started now – read on, quiz yourself and increase your knowledge of Terraria right now!

Best of luck,

James

Contents

Melee Weapons 1

1.) What is the weakest sword in the game?

2.) What is the smallest sword in the game?

3.) How many tin bars do you need to craft a tin shortsword?

4.) The Boreal Wood Sword uses Boreal Wood from what biome?

5.) The Rich Mahogany Sword uses wood from which biome?

6.) How much cactus does it take to make a Cactus Sword?

7.) The Ebonwood Sword uses Ebonwood from which biome?

8.) How many bars of Tungsten does a Tungsten Sword need?

9.) On what scary film is the Bladed Glove based?

10.) What melee weapon does the Stylist use?

Melee Weapons 2

1.) What is the most powerful early game ore broadsword?

2.) What melee weapon does the Traveling Merchant sell?

3.) What biome is the Ice Blade found in?

4.) What is Light's Bane made from?

5.) Name the five Demonite items available to a player

6.) Who drops the Exotic Scimitar?

7.) What is the Blood Butcherer crafted from?

8.) Where can Starfury be obtained from?

9.) The Enchanted Sword being stuck in stone is based on what myth?

10.) What sword does the Queen Bee give up on death?

Melee Weapons 3

1.) What do you need to craft the Phasesaber?

2.) What is the strongest pre-Hardmode sword?

3.) What is the largest sword?

4.) What sword would Pirate enemies drop?

5.) What sword does Plantera drop?

6.) What color are the projectiles from the Beam Sword?

7.) What is Excalibur crafted from?

8.) How is True Excalibur different from Excalibur?

9.) Who drops the Horseman's Blade?

10.) Who drops the Christmas Tree Sword?

Melee Weapons 4

1.) What color projectiles does the Terra Blade emit during a bloodmoon?

2.) What type of bar is the Artery yo-yo crafted from?

3.) Who sells the Code 1 yo-yo?

4.) What type of chests hold the Valor yo-yo?

5.) What is the most powerful, pre-Hardcore, yo-yo?

6.) Who sells the Format: C yo-yo?

7.) Who sells the Code 2 yo-yo?

8.) What is the most powerful yo-yo?

9.) What type of chests would you find the Trident?

10.) Which biome do you need to fish in to find the Swordfish?

Melee Weapons 5

1.) What is the strongest, pre-hardmode, spear?

2.) In what substance must you fish to find the Obsidian Swordfish?

3.) What additional item do you need to obtain the Obsidian Swordfish?

4.) When fired, what does the North Pole spear leave behind?

5.) What type of weapon is Fruitcake Chakram?

6.) Which of the pre-Hardmode boomerangs inflicts the highest damage?

7.) What are Light Discs not allowed to have?

8.) Who drops Bananarangs?

9.) What do you need to craft The Meatball?

10.) When might the KO Cannon be dropped?

Melee Weapons 6

1.) What type of weapon is Dao of Pow?

2.) Who drops Flower Pow?

3.) What is the weakest type of bow?

4.) What is the strongest wooden bow?

5.) Who might drop the Marrow Bow?

6.) Who might drop the Ice Bow?

7.) Who sells the Pulse Bow?

8.) What is the weakest repeater?

9.) Who sells stakes for the Stake Launcher?

10.) What is the only type of named gun model in Terraria that is also in the real world?

1.) Who drops the Chain Gun?

2.) Why is the Grenade Launcher rather strangely named?

3.) Who sells the Proximity Mine Launcher?

4.) Who drops Stynger?

5.) What does the blowpipe use as ammo?

6.) Name the 7 types of Gem Staff

7.) You don't need metal ingots to craft and Amber Staff.

What do you need instead?

8.) What is the strongest staff from the Gem staffs?

9.) Who drops the Blizzard Staff?

10.) Where is the Water Bolt found?

1.) How many melee weapons are there in the game?

2.) What color are the fireballs from the Cursed Flames weapon?

3.) What kind of projectile does the Magical Harp send out?

4.) What is the one block that the Shroomite Digging Claw cannot mine?

5.) What is the War Axe of the Night crafted from?

6.) Who else needs to be present for the Pirate NPC to sell the Bunny Cannon?

7.) What is the blast radius of Dynamite?

8.) The Queen Spider Staff summon the Queen Spider character. How long does she last for?

9.) What minion does the Tempest Staff summon?

10.) Name an anvil at which the Venom Staff can be made.

Armor 1

1.) What are the pre-Hardmode Ore armors?

2.) What is the weakest set of armor?

3.) What is the Crimson version of Ebonwood armor?

4.) What are the two colors or Eskimo Armor?

5.) How much cactus is needed to make Cactus Armor?

6.) What three items make up Ninja Armor?

7.) Which armor has the highest pre-hardmode defense?

8.) Which is the worst Hardmode armor?

9.) Which staff must you have in order to buy Tiki Armor?

10.) In addition to titanium and adamantite bars, what else do

you need to craft Frost Armor?

Armor 2

1.) What appears above your head if wearing a full set of Chlorophyte Armor?

2.) What mode can you enter when wearing Shroomite Armor?

3.) The Wizard Hat increases magic damage by how much?

4.) By how much (%) does the diamond robe reduce mana usage?

5.) In what slot does Gi go in?

6.) What are the default Hardmode ore armors?

7.) Who drops Boots of Ostara?

8.) At which anvils can Titan armor be crafted?

9.) What is the set bonus of Beetle armor?

10.) What is the set bonus of Spooky Armor?

Bosses 1

1.) After King Slime, what is the next biggest slime?

2.) What is the status message when King Slime spawns?

3.) What is the status message when he gets defeated?

4.) How many slimes killed does it take to be killed during Slime Rain for King Slime to appear?

5.) What does King Slime spawn?

6.) What is the achievement called for killing King Slime?

7.) How can you summon Eye of Cthulhu?

8.) What is the status message when it appears automatically?

9.) What is the achievement called for beating Eye of Cthulhu?

10.) What does Eye of Cthulhu spawn?

Bosses 2

1.) What ore does Eye of Cthulhu drop in a Corruption word?

2.) What ore does Eye of Cthulhu drop in a Crimson word?

3.) What is the minimum amount of defense you must have for Eye of Cthulhu to spawn>

4.) How many Shadow Orbs need to be destroyed to summon Eater of Worlds?

5.) How many segments does Eater of Worlds have?

6.) What is the achievement called for beating Eater of Worlds?

7.) How many crimson hearts need to be destroyed for Brain of Cthulhu to spawn?

8.) What item can be used to summon Brain of Cthulhu?

9.) Which environment does Brain of Cthulhu appear in?

10.) What is the achievement called for beating Brain of Cthulhu?

Bosses 3

1.) What areas does the killing of Skeletron allow access to?

2.) How is Skeletron summoned?

3.) What item can also be used to summon Skeletron?

4.) What is the achievement for killing Skeletron called?

5.) Name a weapon gained from beating Queen Bee

6.) What is the achievement called for beating Queen Bee?

7.) What does Queen Bee attack with?

8.) Where does Wall of Flesh spawn?

9.) Where is Wall of Flesh vulnerable?

10.) How is Wall of Flesh summoned?

1.) What are the little mouths on Wall of Flesh called?

2.) What do Wall of Flesh's eyes fire?

3.) What text do you see when Wall of Flesh is beaten?

4.) What happens in the game when Wall of Flesh is beaten?

5.) What is the name of the achievement for beating Wall of Flesh?

6.) What is the name of the achievement for entering Hardmode?

7.) What type of creature is The Destroyed?

8.) What is the name of the achievement for beating The Destroyer?

9.) How many segments does The Destroyer have?

10.) What happens if you don't kill The Destroyer by dawn?

Bosses 5

1.) What item can summon The Destroyer?

2.) What is used to summon Skeletron Prime?

3.) What is the name of the achievement for beating Skeletron Prime?

4.) "This is going to be a terrible night" signal the arrival of what Boss?

5.) How are The Twins summoned?

6.) What are the names of each eye?

7.) Which is the stronger of the two?

8.) What is the name of the achievement for beating The Twins?

9.) What is the name of the achievement for beating 3 Mechanical Bosses?

10.) Which biome does Plantera appear in?

Bosses 6

1.) When Planetera spawns, what is the message?

2.) What is the name of the achievement for beating Plantera?

3.) What does Plantera drop when beaten?

4.) Which NPC becomes available when Plantera is beaten?

5.) Where is Golem found?

6.) Above which altar does Golem spawn?

7.) What is the name of the achievement for beating Golem?

8.) What type of worm is used to summon Duke Fishron?

9.) Which Biome holds Truffle Worms?

10.) How much health does Duke Fishron start with in

Hardcore mode?

Bosses 7

1.) What is the name of the achievement for beating Duke Fishron?

2.) What is the alternative name for Lunatic Cultist?

3.) What is the name of the achievement for beating Lunatic Cultist?

4.) How is Lunatic Cultist summoned?

5.) Beating Lunatic Cultist starts what?

6.) How many Celestial Towers are there?

7.) What text appears with the arrival of Moon Lord?

8.) What item can be used to summon Moon Lord?

9.) What is Moon Lord's max life in Hardcore mode?

10.) What is the name of the achievement for beating Moon Lord?

NPC 1

1.) What does The Angler throw?

2.) What is the name of the achievement for doing the first fishing quest for The Angler?

3.) What must happen for Arms Dealer to spawn?

4.) What weapon does Arms Dealer use in Hardcore mode?

5.) Clothier sells what type of items?

6.) What weapons does Demolitionist use?

7.) How does he spawn?

8.) What weapon does Dye Trader use?

9.) What must be true for the Merchant to spawn?

10.) What weapon does Merchant use?

NPC 2

1.) What is the achievement for spending more than 1 gold coin to be treated by the Nurse?

2.) Who might say "You pathetic fool. You cannot hope to face my master as you are now"

3.) How many other NPCs must be gained before Painter appears?

4.) What does Painter use as a weapon?

5.) What is the percentage chance of Party Girl randomly spawning each morning?

6.) At what time of the day does Skeleton Merchant's stock change?

7.) How many other NPCs must be there for Traveling Merchant to spawn?

8.) What is the percentage chance of Traveling Merchant spawning on a given day?

9.) What does Truffle sell?

10.) What does Truffle fight with?

NPC 3

1.) What is the achievement called when Truffle moves into a House?

2.) Truffle has lots of names (Porcini, Shiitake) – what are they all types of?

3.) What are the dates of the Christmas Season?

4.) How many items can Santa Claus sell?

5.) How many other names does Santa Claus have?

6.) What weapon does Steampunker use?

7.) At what layer can the Wizard NPC be found?

8.) What does Wizard use for a weapon?

9.) Who might say "Not so fast! You got your money, now begone!"

10.) What is Tax Collector's maximum storage?

Buffs

1.) What is the default buff hotkey on a keyboard?

2.) How many active buffs can you have at any points?

3.) What does the Archery buff do?

4.) What does the calming potion do?

5.) What does the fishing potion do?

6.) What does the Gills potion do?

7.) What does the Hunter potion do?

8.) How long does the Rage buff last?

9.) How long does the Summoning buff last?

10.) How long does the Warmth buff last?

Herbs

1.) In what biome would you find blinkroot?

2.) In what biome would you find daybloom?

3.) On what does fireblossom grow?

4.) On what does moonglow grow?

5.) In what biome would you find waterleaf?

6.) In what biome would you find deathweed?

7.) When does deathweed grow?

8.) When does moonglow grow?

9.) On what blocks does cactus grow?

10.) What are the three colors of thorny bushes?

Candles

1.) Which candle increase enemy spawn rate?

2.) Which candle decreases enemy spawn rate?

3.) How many types of metal chandelier are there?

4.) What are the three colors of Christmas Light?

5.) How much does a torch cost to buy?

6.) How do you craft a demon torch?

7.) What color light comes from a cursed torch?

8.) A cursed torch works under water. What is the only other torch that does the same?

9.) Who sells the bone torch?

10.) Who sells the Ultrabright torch?

Fishing

1.) What must you have in your inventory to fish?

2.) How much fishing power does the angler earring add?

3.) How much fishing power does the angler armor add?

4.) How much fishing power does the fishing potion add?

5.) What does the sextant do?

6.) What is the benefit of the High Test Fishing Line?

7.) What does the Fisherman's Pocket Guide show?

8.) What reward do you get when finishing 5 quests for the Angler NPC?

9.) What reward do you get when finishing 15 quests for the Angler NPC?

10.) What reward do you get when finishing 20 quests for the Angler NPC?

Coins / Ores 1

1.) How many copper coins is 1 silver coin worth?

2.) When you die in Softcore mode how many coins from you inventory do you lose?

3.) When you die in Hardcore mode how many coins from you inventory do you lose?

4.) How many types of coin are there?

5.) What is the most valuable type of coin?

6.) Can you craft coins from the materials?

7.) In what weapon can you use coins?

8.) Where are ores normally made into bars?

9.) With what item are ores mined?

10.) What device can turn silt into ore?

Coins / Ores 2

1.) What is the weakest ore?

2.) How much can you sell Tin Ore for?

3.) How much can you sell Iron Ore for?

4.) Iron Ore and what two other ingredients make up Ironskin Potion?

5.) What is the equivalent of Silver Ore?

6.) How many silver coins can you sell Gold Ore for?

7.) What are the ingredients of Spelunker Potion?

8.) How many silver coins can you sell Platinum Ore for?

9.) Which debuff can you get in contact with Meteorite?

10.) What pickaxes will let you mine meteorite?

1.) What could you use instead of a pickaxe to mine meteorite?

2.) What color does Demonite ore show?

3.) Which worlds will Demonite ore not appear in?

4.) Obsidian is formed with the combination of which two things?

5.) What is the minimum pickaxe power needed to mine obsidian?

6.) What are the ingredients of obsidian skin potion?

7.) Where is Hellstone found?

8.) Touching hellstone gives you which debuff?

9.) What is the lowest type of hardmode ore?

10.) How many silver coins will cobalt sell for?

1.) What color is Palladium ore?

2.) What color is orichalcum ore?

3.) What is the rarest ore that spawns from an altar?

4.) Where does chlorophyte ore occur naturally?

5.) What ore does the Moon Lord drop?

6.) What is the achievement for mining your first ore called?

7.) What is the achievement for mining your first hardcore ore called?

8.) What is the achievement for mining your first Chlorophyte called?

9.) Which ores are not shown up by the Spelunker buff?

10.) Which potion does show up Hellstone?

Accessories 1

1.) What does the aglet do?

2.) Where is the amber horseshow balloon crafted?

3.) Where can you find anklet of the wind?

4.) How do you get the balloon pufferfish?

5.) Where do you find blizzard in a bottle?

6.) What does bundle of balloons do?

7.) What does climbing claws do?

8.) Where can you find cloud in a bottle?

9.) What does fart in a jar let you do?

10.) What does flurry boots let you do?

Accessories 2

1.) Where do you find flying carpet?

2.) What does flying carpet let you do?

3.) How might you get frog leg?

4.) What does frog leg do?

5.) What do frostspark boots do?

6.) What does green horseshoe balloon do?

7.) Where do you find Hermes boots?

8.) What do Hermes boots do?

9.) What does Honey balloon release?

10.) Where do you find ice skates?

Accessories 3

1.) Where do you find lava charm?

2.) How many seconds of safety do you get in lava with lava charm?

3.) What does lucky horseshoe do?

4.) Where do you find lucky horseshoe?

5.) What does Master Ninja Gear do?

6.) Who sells rocket boots?

7.) Where do you find sandstorm in a bottle?

8.) Where do you find shiny red balloon?

9.) What do shoe spikes do?

10.) What does Tabi let you do?

Accessories 4

1.) Where would you find water walking boots?

2.) Which anvil would you use to craft wings?

3.) What is special about beetle wings?

4.) Who drops festive wings?

5.) Who gives you Fin Wings as a reward?

6.) Who sells Jetpack?

7.) Who sells leaf wings?

8.) Who sells sparkly wings?

9.) Who sells the ruler?

10.) Who sells the mechanical ruler?

Accessories 5

1.) What does the mechanical ruler do?

2.) Who drops the metal detector?

3.) What does the stopwatch show?

4.) What does DPS stand for in DPS meter?

5.) What does the Tally Counter show?

6.) Who sells the lifeform analyser?

7.) What does the lifeform analyser show you?

8.) What does the band of starpower do?

9.) Who sells the celestial magnet?

10.) What does the mana flower do?

1.) Where does Nature's Gift grow?

2.) Who drops the Philosopher's Stone?

3.) What does Valentine Ring do?

4.) What does adhesive bandage do?

5.) What does ankh charm do?

6.) What does Bezoar do?

7.) Who might drop Bezoar?

8.) Who drops Black Belt?

9.) What does Blindfold do?

10.) Who drops Blindfold?

Accessories 7

1.) Where can you find Cobalt Shield?

2.) What does Cobalt Shield give you?

3.) What does Countercurse Mantra stop happening to you?

4.) Who drops the Cross Necklace?

5.) Who drops Fast Clock?

6.) What does Fast Clock prevent happening to you?

7.) Where do you fund Feral Claws?

8.) What does Feral Claws do?

9.) Who drops Flesh Knuckles?

10.) Who drops Frozen Turtle Shell?

Accessories 8

1.) At what period can you get Hand Warmer?

2.) What does Hercules Beetle do?

3.) Who drops the Magic Quiver?

4.) What does Magic Quiver do?

5.) Who drops the Megaphone?

6.) What does Megaphone do?

7.) Who drops the Moon Stone?

8.) What does Nazar stop?

9.) Who drops Ranger Emblem?

10.) How much defense does Shackle add?

1.) How much extra magic damage does Sorcerer Emblem

provide?

2.) What does Titan Glove do?

3.) What does Extendo Grip do?

4.) What does Portable Cement Mixer increase?

5.) What does Brick Layer increase?

6.) What does yo-yo Glove do?

7.) What does Coin Ring do?

8.) Where can you find flower boots?

9.) Who drops the Gold Ring?

10.) What does Jellyfish Necklace do?

Accessories 10

1.) What does string do to a yo-yo?

2.) Who drops the moon charm?

3.) What does the Necromantic Scroll do?

4.) Who sells Music Box?

5.) In what type of crate would you find Ginger Beard?

6.) How much do the cloaks from Traveling Merchant cost?

7.) Name the three types of cape you can buy

8.) How much does the Diamond Ring cost?

9.) Who drops the Necromantic Scroll?

10.) Who drops Lucky Coin?

Biomes 1

1.) What layer does the Underground Snow biome start?

2.) Which debuffs are Armored Vikings immune to?

3.) How does Ice Tortoise attack?

4.) What is the first layer below the surface?

5.) What is the greatest number of segments Giant Worm will have?

6.) What type of chest holds Jester's Arrows?

7.) What is the largest layer?

8.) Where can you find Bee Hive?

9.) Which blocks hold Floating Lakes?

10.) How many Harpies can be on screen during a Blood Moon?

Biomes 2

1.) What is the name of the achievement for finding a Floating Island?

2.) What is the one environment that Corruption and Crimson don't spread?

3.) Who tells you how much, in percentage, there is of Hallow and Corruption or Crimson?

4.) How much mining power does a pickaxe need to mine Lihzahrd Bricks?

5.) Where is the Flame Trap found?

6.) Which buff alerts you about traps?

7.) What is the achievement called for getting killed by a trap for the first time?

8.) How much more (in general) damage do you suffer from traps in expert mode?

9.) What is the tree type contained in the Ocean biome?

10.) Who sells the Beach Ball?

Debuffs 1

1.) What color do you turn when poisoned?

2.) What color do you turn with the Venom debuff?

3.) What does the bleeding debuff stop you doing?

4.) What does the darkness debuff do?

5.) What does the silenced debuff do?

6.) What does the cursed debuff do?

7.) Which buff negates the Weak debuff?

8.) By how much is armor reduced with the Broken Armor debuff?

9.) What color do you glow the Ichor debuff?

10.) Which debuff slows down your speed?

Debuffs 2

1.) Which debuff burns you with cursed flames?

2.) How long do you drip water for with the Wet debuff?

3.) Which debuff changes gravity?

4.) Which debuff makes you stay where you are?

5.) Which debuff do you not want to get when fighting Wall of Flesh?

6.) Which debuff removes so much light you can't really see anything?

7.) How long does Potion Sickness last for?

8.) Mana sickness reduces your magic damage by how much?

9.) What color fumes surround you with the Stinky debuff?

10.) What color do you turn with Slime debuff?

Debuffs 3

1.) Who can cancel debuffs?

2.) How much does it cost to cancel one debuff?

3.) What happens with the Confused debuff?

4.) What happens with the Horrified debuff?

5.) How much defense do you lose with the Ichor debuff?

6.) What does the electrified debuff do?

7.) Using what item makes you lose life with the Chaos State debuff?

8.) How long does the Tipsy debuff last for?

9.) How can you put out fire?

10.) Which debuff does the tooltip "You are completely petrified" signify?

Mounts 1

1.) Which key on the keyboard summons a mount item?

2.) How many mount types are there?

3.) What does the achievement "The Cavalry" signify?

4.) Slimy Saddle increases your movement speed by how much?

5.) Which mount does Honeyed Goggles summon?

6.) Once the bee becomes tired, how long does it need to rest on the ground?

7.) What does the Hardy Saddle summon?

8.) What does the Fuzzy Carrot summon?

9.) What does the Pigron Mount let you do?

10.) What summons Pigron Mount?

Mounts 2

1.) What does the Shrimpy Truffle summon?

2.) What can Cute Fishron do forever?

3.) What does Reindeer Bells summon?

4.) Which boss might drop Reindeer Bells

5.) What does Cosmic Car Key summon?

6.) Who drops UFO Mount?

7.) In what does the UFO Mount not work?

8.) What does Brain Scrambler summon?

9.) What does Blessed Apple summon?

10.) What is the Rainbows and Unicorns achievement awarded

for?

Achievements 1

1.) Chopping down a tree for the first time gives you which achievement?

2.) Building a house for an NPC gives you which achievement?

3.) Gaining your first hammer gives you which achievement?

4.) Getting an anvil from iron or lead gives you which achievement?

5.) What is Hold on Tight! awarded for?

6.) What is Eye on You awarded for?

7.) What is Sting Operation awarded for?

8.) Smashing a demon or crimson altar with a hammer gives you what achievement?

9.) What is Head in the Clouds awarded for?

10.) Eating a life fruit gives you what achievement?

Achievements 2

1.) Beating the Ancient Cultist gives you what achievement?

2.) What achievement do you get for surviving a blood moon?

3.) What do you get for surviving the slime rain?

4.) If you get every possible town NPC what achievement do you get?

5.) Wandering into a spider caven gives you what achievement?

6.) Smashing 10,000 tiles gives you what achievement?

7.) Throwing lines is awarded for throwing what item?

8.) What do you get for equipping a minishark

9.) What do you get for getting a rainbow rod?

10.) Defeating every single boss gives you what achievement?

Miscellaneous 1

1.) Who drops the Life Drain?

2.) Who sells the Flower Wall?

3.) How much extra defense does Dryad's Blessing award?

4.) What is the weakest arrow in the game?

5.) When do zombies appear?

6.) When is the only time zombies can open doors?

7.) What does the Nymph transform from when you get close?

8.) What is the achievement for killing a nymph for the first time?

9.) Which debuffs are Rune Wizards immune to?

10.) Who can appear with the name Gnudar?

Miscellaneous 2

1.) Where might the Lac Beetle spawn?

2.) What does the Lac Beetle drop on dying?

3.) What is the use of an umbrella?

4.) What has the highest base damage of all the bullets?

5.) What might drop the Buccaneer costume?

6.) What might drop the Picksaw?

7.) Where is the shadow chest found?

8.) Killing a dungeon slime will give you what?

9.) Where is the Basilisk enemy found?

10.) How much health does the Lesser Healing Potion restore?

1.) How much does Confetti cost?

2.) When will the Mood Lord despawn?

3.) What debuffs might Ice Bat give you?

4.) Who sells the Disco Ball?

5.) How long does the Shine buff last for?

6.) What is the knockback value of Slap Hand?

7.) Who sells Slap Hand?

8.) What do sunflowers stop?

9.) Where does the Recall Potion take you?

10.) How many types of Goblin enemy are there?

Melee Weapons 1 Answers

1.) Copper Shortsword

2.) Tiny Copper Shortsword

3.) 7

4.) Snow Biome

5.) Jungle Biome

6.) 10

7.) Corruption Biome

8.) 6

9.) Nightmare on Elm Street

10.) Stylish Scissors

Melee Weapons 2 Answers

1.) Platinum Broadsword

2.) Katana

3.) Underground Snow

4.) Demonite

5.) Light's Ban, Demon Bow, War Axe of the Night, Fisher of Souls, Malaise

6.) The Dye Trader

7.) Crimtane Bars

8.) Skyware Chests or Sky Crates

9.) King Arthur and Merlin

10.) Bee Keeper

Melee Weapons 3 Answers

1.) A Phaseblade and 50 Crystal Shards

2.) Night's Edge

3.) Breaker Blade

4.) Cutlass

5.) Seedler

6.) Gold

7.) Hallowed Bars

8.) It does not auto-swing

9.) Pumpking

10.) Everscreams

Melee Weapons 4 Answers

1.) Orange

2.) Crimtane

3.) Travelling Merchant

4.) Gold Chests

5.) Cascade

6.) Skeleton Merchant

7.) Traveling Merchant

8.) The Terrarian

9.) Underwater

10.) Ocean biome

Melee Weapons 5 Answers

1.) Dark Lance

2.) Lava

3.) Hotline Fishing Hook

4.) Snowflakes

5.) Boomerang

6.) Flamarang

7.) Modifiers

8.) Clowns

9.) Crimtane Bars and Tissue Samples

10.) In a Blood Moon (in Hardmode)

1.) Flail

2.) Plantera

3.) Wooden Bow

4.) Pearlwood

5.) Skeleton Archers

6.) Ice Mimics

7.) Traveling Merchant

8.) Cobalt Repeater

9.) Witch Doctor and Arms Dealer

10.) Uzi

Melee Weapons 7 Answers

1.) Santa-NK1

2.) It doesn't fire grenades

3.) Cyborg NPC

4.) Golem

5.) Seeds or Darts

6.) Amethyst, Topaz, Sapphire, Emerald, Amber, Ruby, Diamond

7.) Sturdy Fossils

8.) Diamond

9.) Ice Queen

10.) In dungeons

Melee Weapons 8 Answers

1.) 143

2.) Green

3.) Musical notes

4.) Lihzahrd Bricks

5.) Demonite Bars

6.) Party Girl

7.) 14 feet or 7 blocks

8.) 2 minutes

9.) Sharknado

10.) Mythril or Orichalcum Anvil

Armor 1 Answers

1.) Copper, Iron, Silver, Gold, Tin, Lead, Tungsten, Platinum

2.) Wooden

3.) Shadewood

4.) Pink and Blue

5.) 75

6.) Ninja Hood, Ninja Shirt, Ninja Pants

7.) Molten

8.) Pearlwood

9.) Pygmy Staff

10.) Frost Core

Armor 2 Answers

1.) A leaf

2.) Stealth Mode

3.) 15%

4.) 15%

5.) Shirt

6.) Cobalt, Mythril, Adamantite

7.) Lepus

8.) Mythril / Orichalcum

9.) Increases melee damage and speed

10.) Extra minion damage

Bosses 1 Answers

1.) Rainbow Slime

2.) "King Slime has awoken!"

3.) "King Slime has been defeated!"

4.) 150

5.) Smaller, blue slimes

6.) Slippery Shinobi

7.) With a Suspicious Looking Eye at Night

8.) "You feel an evil presence watching you"

9.) Eye on You

10.) Servants of Cthulhu

Bosses 2 Answers

1.) Demonite

2.) Crimtane

3.) 10

4.) 3

5.) 50

6.) Worm Fodder

7.) 3

8.) Bloody Spine

9.) Crimson

10.) Mastermind

Bosses 3 Answers

1.) All dungeon areas

2.) Talking to Old Man at entrance to Dungeon at night

3.) Clothier Voodoo Doll

4.) Boned

5.) Bee Keeper, Bee Gun, The Bee's Knees

6.) Sting Operation

7.) Poisonous stingers

8.) Underworld

9.) Eyes or Mouth

10.) Drop Voodoo Doll into lava

Bosses 4 Answers

1.) The Hungry

2.) Lasers

3.) The Ancient Spirits of Light and Dark have been Released

4.) Hardmode entered

5.) Still Hungry

6.) It's Hard

7.) A big worm

8.) Ride the Worm

9.) 82

10.) It despawns

Bosses 5 Answers

1.) Mechanical Worm

2.) Mechanical Skull

3.) Bona Fide

4.) The Twins

5.) Using mechanical eye at night

6.) Retinazer and Spazmatism

7.) Spazmatism

8.) Opthalmologist

9.) Buckets of Bolts

10.) Undeground Jungle

Bosses 6 Answers

1.) Plantera has awoken!

2.) The Great Southern Plantkill

3.) Grenade Launcher

4.) Cyborg

5.) Jungle Temple

6.) Lihzahrd

7.) Lihzahrdian Idol

8.) Truffle Worm

9.) Mushroom

10.) 60,000

Bosses 7 Answers

1.) Fish Out of Water

2.) Ancient Cultist

3.) Obsessive Devotion

4.) Killing the cultists at the Dungeon's entrance

5.) Lunar Events

6.) 4

7.) Impending doom approaches?

8.) Celestial Sigil

9.) 217,500

10.) Champion of Terraria

NPC Answers 1

1.) Frost Daggerfish

2.) Servant-in-Training

3.) Empty House + one Gun or Bullet in inventory

4.) Minishark

5.) Vanity

6.) Grenades

7.) Empty House + explosive in inventory + Merchant alive

8.) Exotic Scimitar

9.) Empty House + all players more than 50 silver coins

10.) Throwing Knives

NPC Answers 2

1.) The Frequent Flyer

2.) Old Man

3.) 8

4.) Paintball gun

5.) 2.5%

6.) 4:30am

7.) 2

8.) 25%

9.) Autohammer

10.) Mushroom spores

NPC Answers 2

1.) It Can Talk!?

2.) Mushroom

3.) December 15-31

4.) 39

5.) 0

6.) Clockwork Assault Rifle

7.) Cavern

8.) Fireballs

9.) Tax Collector

10.) 10 Gold Coins

Buffs Answers

1.) B

2.) 22

3.) Arrow speed and damage up by 20%

4.) Enemy NPC spawn rate decrease

5.) Fishing power goes up

6.) Let player breathe underwater

7.) Let player find enemy NPCs more easily

8.) 4 minutes

9.) 6 minutes

10.) 25 minutes

Herbs Answers

1.) Underground

2.) Surface

3.) Ash

4.) Jungle grass

5.) Desert

6.) Corruption / Crimson

7.) In a blood moon or full moon

8.) During the night

9.) Sand blocks

10.) Brown / Purple / Red

Candles Answers

1.) Water Candle

2.) Peace Candle

3.) 6

4.) Blue, Red Green

5.) 50 Copper coins

6.) Add together standard torch with obsidian

7.) Green

8.) Ichor Torch

9.) Skeleton Merchant

10.) Traveling Merchant

Fishing Answers

1.) Bait

2.) 10

3.) 5 per piece

4.) 15

5.) Displays the phase of the moon

6.) Line never breaks

7.) Current fishing power

8.) Fuzzy Carrot

9.) Angler Vest

10.) Angler Pants

Coins / Ores Answers 1

1.) 100

2.) Half

3.) All of them

4.) 4

5.) Platinum

6.) No

7.) Coin Gun

8.) At a furnace

9.) Pickaxe

10.) Extractinator

Coins / Ores Answers 2

1.) Copper / Tin

2.) 75 Copper coins

3.) 1 silver coin

4.) Bottled Water + Daybloom

5.) Tungsten Ore

6.) 4

7.) Gold or Platinum Ore , Bottled Water, Blinkroot + Moonglow

8.) 6

9.) Burning

10.) Tungsten, Gold, Platinum

1.) Explosives

2.) Blue

3.) Crimson

4.) Water and lava

5.) 65%

6.) Obsidian, waterleaf, fireblossom, bottled water

7.) Underworld

8.) Burning

9.) Cobalt

10.) 7

1.) Orange

2.) Purple-ish

3.) Adamantite

4.) Undgerground jungle

5.) Luminite

6.) Ooo! Shiny!

7.) Extra Shiny!

8.) Photosynthesis

9.) Hellstone and Obsidian

10.) Dangersense Potion

Accessories 1 Answers

1.) Increase speed

2.) Tinkerer's workshop

3.) Underground jungle shrines

4.) Fish for it!

5.) Ice chests

6.) Increases jump height

7.) Slide down walls

8.) Underground / Cavern chests

9.) Double jump

10.) Run at double speed

Accessories 2 Answers

1.) Pyramid chests

2.) Float (briefly)

3.) Through fishing

4.) Increase jump speed

5.) Faster running and extra mobility

6.) Allow double jump

7.) Underground chests

8.) Let you run at double speed

9.) Bees

10.) Ice chests

Accessories 3 Answers

1.) Underground gold chests

2.) 7

3.) Remove fall damage

4.) Floating islands chests

5.) Climb walls and dodge attacks

6.) Goblin Tinkerer

7.) Pyramid chests

8.) Floating islands chests

9.) Slide down walls jump

10.) Dash

1.) Water chests

2.) Mythril

3.) Silent

4.) Everscream

5.) Angler

6.) Steampunker

7.) Witch doctor

8.) Dryad

9.) Goblin tinkerer

10.) Mechanic

Accessories 5 Answers

1.) Shows measurement lines on the screen

2.) Nymph

3.) How fast you are moving

4.) Damager Per Second

5.) Number of monsters killed

6.) Traveling Merchant

7.) The name of the creature near you

8.) Increases max mana by 20

9.) Traveling Merchant

10.) Reduces the mana usage by 8%

Accessories 6 Answers

1.) Underground jungle?

2.) Mimic

3.) Regenerates health by 50%

4.) Prevents bleeding

5.) Gives you protection from the majority of debuffs

6.) Gives you protection from poison

7.) Hornet or Toxic Sludge

8.) Bone Lee

9.) See in the darkness

10.) Corrupt Slime / Dark Mummy

Accessories 7 Answers

1.) Dungeon Chests

2.) Prevents you suffering knockback

3.) Silenced or Cursed

4.) Mimic

5.) Pixie

6.) Slows

7.) Underground Jungle Shrines

8.) Increase melee speed

9.) Crimson Mimic

10.) Ice Tortoise

Accessories 8 Answers

1.) Christmas

2.) Increases the damage caused by minions

3.) Skeleton Archer

4.) Increases the speed and damage by arrows

5.) Pixie

6.) Stops you being silenced

7.) Vampire

8.) You being cursed

9.) Wall of Flesh

10.) 1

Accessories 9 Answers

1.) 15%

2.) Knockback goes up

3.) Tile reach goes up by 3

4.) Wall placement speed

5.) Tile placement speed

6.) Lets you use 2 yo-yos at the same time

7.) Increases your coin pickup range

8.) Jungle Shrines chests

9.) Flying Dutchman

10.) Gives you light under the water

1.) Range increase

2.) Werewolf

3.) Increase max number of minions allowed

4.) Wizard

5.) Iron

6.) 5 gold coins

7.) Winter, Mysterious + Red

8.) 2 Platinum coins

9.) Mourning Wood

10.) Pirate

Biomes 1 Answers

1.) Cavern

2.) Poisoned / Venom

3.) Spinning and Jumping

4.) Underground

5.) 8

6.) Gold

7.) Cavern

8.) Underground Jungle

9.) Cloud + Rain

10.) 15

Biomes 2 Answers

1.) Is This Heaven?

2.) The Hallow

3.) The Dryad

4.) 210

5.) Jungle Temple

6.) Dangersense

7.) Watch Your Step!

8.) Double the damage

9.) Palm Wood

10.) Party Girl

Debuffs 1 Answers

1.) Green

2.) Purple

3.) Regenerating life

4.) Lessens the brightness so you can't see as much

5.) Using anything with mana

6.) Using anything

7.) Werewolf

8.) Half

9.) Yellow

10.) Chilled

Debuffs 2 Answers

1.) Cursed Inferno

2.) 30 seconds

3.) Distorted

4.) Webbed

5.) The Tongue

6.) Blackout

7.) 1 minute

8.) 25%

9.) Green

10.) Blue

Debuffs 3 Answers

1.) Nurse

2.) 7 Silver + 50 Copper coins

3.) Keyboard movement keys are reversed

4.) A warning to stop you leaving Underworld

5.) 20

6.) Suffer big damage when moving

7.) Rod of Discord

8.) 2 minutes

9.) Leap into a water pool

10.) Stoned

Mounts 1 Answers

1.) R

2.) 11

3.) Equipping your first mount

4.) 20mph

5.) Bee Mount

6.) 3 seconds

7.) Turtle Mount

8.) Bunny

9.) Fly and run faster on land

10.) Scaly Truffle

Mounts 2 Answers

1.) Cute Fishron

2.) Fly

3.) Rudloph

4.) Ice Queen

5.) UFO Mount

6.) Martian Saucer

7.) Any form of liquid

8.) Scutlix Mount

9.) Unicorn

10.) Shooting a Rainbow Gun + riding a Unicorn

Achievements 1 Answers

1.) Timber

2.) No Hobo

3.) Stop! Hammer Time!

4.) Heavy Metal

5.) Equipping your first grappling hook

6.) Beating Eye of Cthulhu

7.) Beating Queen Bee

8.) Begone, Evil!

9.) Equiping a pair of wings

10.) Get a Life

Achievements 2 Answers

1.) Obsessive Devotion

2.) Bloodbath

3.) Sticky Situation

4.) Real Estate Agent

5.) Jeepers Creepers

6.) Bulldozer

7.) Yo-yo

8.) Completely awesome

9.) Prismancer

10.) Slayer of Worlds

1.) Crimson Mimic

2.) Dryad

3.) 8

4.) Wooden Arrow

5.) At night

6.) During a blood moon

7.) Lost Girl

8.) Deceiver of Fools

9.) Poisoned and venom

10.) Goblin Tinkerer

Miscellaneous 2 Answers

1.) Underground Jungle

2.) Violet Husk

3.) Slowing a fall

4.) Luminite Bullet

5.) Pirate Invasion enemy

6.) Golem

7.) Underworld

8.) Golden key

9.) Underground Desert

10.) 50

Miscellaneous 3 Answers

1.) 1 silver coin

2.) When all players die

3.) Chilled or Frozen

4.) Merchant

5.) 5 minutes

6.) 20

7.) Skeleton Merchant

8.) Corruption

9.) Back to your spawn point

10.) 7

36645906R00061

Made in the USA
Middletown, DE
07 November 2016